I0608499

Love, Island

For Lotus

6/14/1947 – 1/18/2021

Love, Island

Poems by Sandra Noel

Goldfish Press, Seattle

Copyright © 2021 Goldfish Press,
an imprint of Chrysanthemum Publications, Inc.

All rights reserved. No part of this publication may be
reproduced, distributed, or transmitted in any form or by any
means, including photocopying, recording, or other electronic or
mechanical methods, without the prior permission of the
publisher, except in case of brief quotation embodied in critical
reviews and certain other noncommercial uses permitted by
copyright law.

For permission requests, write to us at the address below.

ISBN 13:   978-1-950276-14-1
ISBN 10:   1-950276-14-7

Library of Congress Catalog Control Number: 2021931028

Book Design by Susan Steiner using Aparajita Typeface

Cover Photo: "Web Poem" © 2013 by Jean Mead

Cover Design: Noel Design, LLC

Goldfish Press is a literary press of all genres.

Goldfish Press
4545 42nd Ave. SW
Suite 211
Seattle, WA 98116

Acknowledgements:

"Heron," Buddhist Poetry Review, Issue III, 2011,"Reefnet Summer," Elohi Gadugi Journal, Indigenous Issue, 2012, "Stone and Bone," Elohi Gadugi Journal, Narratives for a New World, Volume 1, 2013, "Star Craft," Chrysanthemum Literary Anthology, 2020, "Drift I, II and III," Bellowing Arc, Issue #3, 2020, "The Weight of Water," "How Can I Feel Uninspired," Bellowing Arc, Issue #2, 2020, "Sacrifice," "In the Wetland," "Reeds I and II," The Gypsy in my Kitchen, chapbook, July, 2015, Finishing Line Press, "One," "Hold a Stone," "Sunrise on Fisher Pond," "What I see, What I Hear," chapbook, 2017, Into the Green, Finishing Line Press, "A Thousand Moons," Following the Drift," chapbook, Unraveling the Endless Knot, 2019, Middle Creek Publishing and Audio

Table of Contents:

Once Upon an Island

Return Again   2
Once Upon an Island   3
Reefnet Summer   4-6
The Song in my Heart   7
Love, Island   8
Blackberry Summer   9
Place   10-11
After a Friend from College Asked   12
Paradise Found   13
In this Light at the End of the Day   14
Rowers on Quartermaster   15
Summer on the Loop   16
Ghost Mountain, Mount Rainier   17

In the Wetland

A broken Heart has Wings   19
In the Wetland   20
The Wave of Forever   21
Sacrifice   22
Some Days   23
You, Me, and the Rain   24

Point Robinson Beach   25

Counting my Blessings   26

How to Love Simply, Without Judgement   27

The House of Joy   28

Heron   29

Windrows on Mukai Pond   30

All we can Hold   31

Reeds I   32

Reeds II   33

The Alchemy of Rain

Running in the Rain   35

The Alchemy of Rain   36

The Weight of Water   37

At the Edge of the World   38

One   39-40

Sunrise on Fisher Pond   41

Form Follows Function   42

The Lives of Stones   43

I Want to be Lost   44

Stone and Bone   45-46

Hold a Stone   47

What I See, What I hear   48

On the Trail this Morning   49

Come Early   50

How Can I Feel Uninspired?   51

Mukai Pond Before the Rains   52

A Thousand Moons

Loons   54

This Business of Survival   55

Transpiration   56

Drift I   57

Drift II   58

Drift III   59

A Thousand Moons   60

Following the Drift   61

Between   62

Star Craft   63

Red Tide   64

At the Lighthouse   65

After Reading Mary Oliver's Thirst and Pondering
Faith   66

Once Upon an Island

Return Again

Save me the dried apples
save me the sweet jam
made from last summer's blackberries
for I will return again
always to this island
where light silvers over
the wide bay
morning and evening
and wild voices call me
awake and to sleep
from the trees and the open air
I will always return
even as bones and dust
to rest at last
by this quiet shore.

Once Upon an Island

We were American refugees
huddled around our wood stoves
drinking wine and smoking pot
over cribbage and conversation
too young to think beyond
the next day's fishing.
Some did not survive
to the old age we feared
the rest of us are left
to remember
setting the boats on buoys
waiting for the tide
to lift us all
and bring the salmon
those great wily wild ones
into our leads and nets.
Nothing I have done since
has been done with such abandon
not even love.

Reefnet Summer (For Captain Buffy, the salmon slayer)

Until you sent the photograph of the two of us
standing together on the beach, dressed to kill
in our heavy natty woolen sweaters
glittering in dry fish scales
I'd forgotten that summer we spent
waiting on the floodtide to bring
the salmon moving northward toward the Fraser
listening to gulls and herons
and the low talk of the men on the outside sets
who laughed and hooted like teenagers
when we'd pee in an old Maxwell House can
and tossed its contents over the low gunnels.
We stood on slapstick-welded towers
20 feet above swaying decks, the metal rungs
slick with fish slime and morning mist
stared through glare-free sunglasses
into the dark water of the small bay
waiting for sockeyes, chums, silvers, humpies
and the occasional kings – money fish
to make their way up the sidelines
and into our empty pockets.
We waited, patiently, quietly
women know how to wait
a skill embedded in our DNA
for our men at work or at war

for a difficult birth or a slow death.
So suddenly they'd appear
glimmering, smooth torpedo-shaped and moving fast!
No time to say, "Beautiful!" but we'd all think it
and from deep in our throats - a blood call,
"GIVER ER HELL!"
high pitched, wild women screams!
Then, half-stumbling, drunk on adrenaline
rushed down to the decks below.
I remember your speed and timing
as you deftly worked the winches
and helped us haul in the net, heavy with fish
your gentle strength as you carried the big kings
lovingly, like wriggling, defiant two-year olds
from the tangle of net on deck
to the slushy ice water of the hold
for the buyer boat with their scale
and handfuls of cash at the end of the day.
There were orcas, almost close enough to touch
more than once on the ride back to the beach
eying our uncounted dinner
loaded in the small skiff at dusk
back to that lonely little island
lost now to tourism and real estate developers
where you helped me gain strength enough
to leave a bad marriage and raise a good son
where I learned a dying trade
and found my ancient female voice

the one I'd lost a few years earlier
when a stranger in the darkness
dared me to speak, so I lay silent
the scream caught in my throat.

The Song in my Heart

I am grateful
for this place
surrounded by familiar things
it has softened me, yes
but it has also repaired
the broken places.

When a wild bird is mending
you must leave it for a time
in a dark, safe place
surrounded by silence
until it is possible
if it is possible
to be healed
and released again
into the sky.

Love, Island

My Beloved
I know how you came here
but each morning I will give you
love eternal.

Each day I will bring you
sunshine and sunset
osprey and eagle
Do you know how much
I love you?

Come, walk in my forests.
I will embrace you with branches
of sweet-scented cedar
and offerings of salmonberries
in the spring.

Blackberry Summer

The pond is rising
the path we walked
erased by a spring flood.
If the past could be so...
left covered at least a season
when I would not think of summer
and then of you remembering
your full mouth, an empty pail
discarded for momentary sweetness.

I will wander back the long way around
let the misty light soften my thoughts.
After all this still exists
and I have every day to wander
or most days here alone.

Even with you heavy on my heart
there is a lightness too
in the opening sky
the widening pond.

Place

This island born of ice fingers
reaching down from Canada
rests in the middle
of an inland sea
where a people lived
6,000 years before
bones and stone tools
still wash from glacial till
in storm tides.

Cedar stumps carry scars
from springboard notches
when all the trees
ALL the trees
were cut down
to build communities
and clear the land for farms
where Japanese families
grew strawberries
until they were moved to camps
to wait out a war they did not start.

This island
born of ice fingers
Resting in the middle
of an inland sea

where I came to rest
blown by a hard wind
westward to this place.

After a Friend from College Asked

What I had been up to all these years;

Oh
Following the wrong muse
down one rabbit hole
after another.

Winding up on this island
watching an osprey
from a window in my soul.

Paradise Found

On a small island in the Salish Sea
on the west coast of north America
where there are rain forests
and rivers and streams and beaches
this is idealized nonsense
there are also houses and sewers
and clear cuts and dams
but within this is my heart
beating in rhythm
with the tides and moon cycles.
We can make it better
and if we cannot fix it
we can wake up each day
with that idea anyway.

In this Light at the End of the Day

The bay glass-calm
holds a handful of waterfowl
loons glide by in pairs
a pas de deux
and geese in flotillas
kingfishers tear the air above.
What a show and not to be missed
so we pull up our lawn chairs
newly washed of cobwebs
to watch until the sun is low
and the moon rises.

Rowers on Quartermaster Harbor

This morning on the fog-layered bay
rowing shell bow and stern lights
appear as tandem fireflies gliding together
the sound of long oars touch and go
in unison as rowers sleeked through the dark water
one voice calling a count from the coxswain's seat
"Power 10 to 20! Let it run!"
swallowed by distance
as they coursed around the point
and out of reach of my hearing.
Mornings have always come like gifts
a good cup of coffee
and I am born again before first light
when anything is possible
and (almost) anything can be endured.

Summer on the Loop

Bat flits in
through the open window
a silent shadow
finishing his commute
just before sunrise
past my place in bed
in this house
that is like a selfish lover
asking for more and more
money for repairs
than is reasonable
but we want her
so we pay
just to lie between cool sheets
in the morning
like this morning
before the heat of summer
drives us up and out
to our labors
Bat is at work already
in the cobwebs
in the untended corners
of our lives.

Ghost Mountain, Mount Rainier

5 a.m. on the dock
to the southeast
Tahoma, Mother of Waters
rests on the horizon
snow covered clavicle of ice
jutting out over the bay
lights from refineries
glow in the distance
rotting glaciers
down to stone.

In the Wetland

A Broken Heart has Wings

Ravens spin rain silk circles overhead
as we slow slog below
careful of the slick clay beneath our feet
grateful the rain has slowed to mist
grateful we have time for this.

It is here where my heart found wings
among the impossible trees
and raven and owl and osprey
lifted my heavy heart
made the way light for a while
long enough to open up
feel the rain on my face
and let go a little into the wider world.

That's all it takes, really
space and time
and a good dog too maybe...

In the Wetland

Reeds are dying down to brown chaff
fountains of white seed pods from cattails
float on a light breeze.

This is the golden time
the time of folding in and under.
It has been a hard year.
I welcome dormancy
and a long winter's sleep--
this of course is not possible.

I'll go back to the world in a while
but now the redwings are out
and if I am very lucky
no one will come down the trail
without feathers or fur
until the sun is well overhead
and it is time to go.

The Wave of Forever

The cold feels clean
my breath evident
walking over the rise
towards the valley of the firs.
If I close my eyes
the cold creeps into my bones
asking for more
but I am not ready to answer
though somehow
with your quiet passing
it does not seem mysterious.

We live and we die
the deer carcass beside the road
an old cedar stump.

Through the crystalline fields
diminutive marsh wrens rise like a shout
disturbed from their cold retreats
by my passing.
We are a small ripple
through the great wave of forever.

Sacrifice

The day after…
stillness comes
it's the same trail
I ran yesterday
the same moss covers
the dead tree branches.

A small rain creates concentric magic
on the surface of the pond
as a pair of red tails circle overhead
patrolling the parameters
with serial grace.
I offer up my heart to them
broken as it is
as a sacrifice to Horus.

I will go forth singing
in the ancient way
with the old joy
and sweet grace of the body.
This is what I trust
and all know
about anything.
I came here closed
and broken
I leave filled with light.

Some Days

On an evening like this
silence hangs over the bay
bathed in golden light
until the soft rush of wings
it's the heron, right on time
returning to his perch in the fir tree
I count on this if nothing else
some days.

You, Me, and the Rain

The fog rolls down
and covers the trail
rain has softened everything
even my resolve
to never think of you.

I am wet and cold
but exultant in my body
grateful for this ability
to move again with grace
but with it has come
your presence.

I do not understand
but accept
as I do the startling orange
of witch jelly on a dead log.

I wish you happiness
this is true
though you may not believe it
I always wished you this-
my heart break, my joy.

Point Robinson Beach

The tide rolls in
stones dance
over the shore
music waves water
I could sit here all day
on this log
once a great cedar
now bleached and stranded
if I stay long enough
my bones would become
part of the architecture.

All this busy work I do
missing the voices
the music of the earth
and what could be
more important
but I know I will rise
and go back to it
like a worn-out love affair
one foot in, one out.

Counting my Blessings

I woke to a book of poems

and the heron

rising from her fir tree roost

felt my heart open

and a small sad bird fly out.

How to Love Simply, without Judgment

This is uneasy advice
but I know a way to practice.
Walk into a forest
gaze up at the crowns
of tall trees overhead
they breathe in
what we pollute
and breathe out good air.
Look down at the roots
holding the earth
under your feet.
Love a tree
then try the harder stuff.

The House of Joy

Hawk holds the light
in her eye
passing overhead
wingless we wait below
for she has captured our hearts
with her slow arc
we are stilled as prey
before the strike.

Live in the house of joy!
sings the marsh wren
just a few feet away
in the bare brambles
beside the pond
black with early morning
while we sit together
dog and I
my head full of thoughts
his full of joy.

Heron

Prehistoric vocalizations
in the giant fir next to my window
stuttering, shape shifting, lifting
silently soaring across the mirror-black bay
a perfect crescent moon
light on the horizon
first rose, now golden
as I sit on my cushion
with altar and bowl
the first of many habits
acquired with age
to replace the passions
of my youth–only you remain.
I still wake up loving you
knowing you are impossible
(knowing you are impossible!)
I sit and wait for peace to descend
for hope to expire
or rest in a tree nearby
knowing (somehow)
I will never wake to an empty heart
but stagger with the weight of you
each morning
then soar silently into the light.

Windrows on Mukai Pond

I follow the trail
down past the turn-about
to Mukai Pond
as shadows of two Canada geese
glide across its mirror-black surface
and I find a seat on a rough bench
to watch winter ducks and the heron.

The green is almost too much
and then a breeze rolls across
the water's surface carrying light with it
windrows of bright stars
towards the shore
and all I can do is give thanks
for this moment.

All we can Hold

We left early
ahead of the sun
in need of what a sunrise
over still water provides
the best kind of medicine
for soul and body
all troubles melt
at least for those few moments
into the fading darkness.
So much beauty and worry
cannot be held in the heart
simultaneously.

Reeds I

Where are you
with your reed breath
and remarkable eyes
foretold or forewarned in myths
seeking you and only you
I have stumbled over stones
and the bodies of others who came before
because like me they heard
that thin sweet sound
carried on a warm wind one evening
and were compelled to follow
unprepared without a plan
into the dark places
not fearless but determined
seeking outside
what is only found within.
(I know this now
but do not regret the journey.)

Reeds II

I wandered
through the rain-soaked reeds
this morning
watched
as a million insects
flushed from their shelter
flew into the misty light
felt the soft tassels brush my hands
waist deep in the open field
heard singing
yes, I am sure of it
and knew that voice
and loved as I always do the song
as I love the song of the chorus frogs
where the reeds open onto the pond
and nothing matters now
but this understanding
it explains everything
(Nothing is ever lost, not really.)

The Alchemy of Rain

Running in the Rain

Red tail hawk spins overhead

    hunting the fields beside the road.

We go about our business

    even in the rain.

The Alchemy of Rain

As a slate-colored afternoon
refracts into evening
porch light becomes halo.

The sound is soft on the cedars
silent on the bay from this distance
as the heron gives up his ground
arcs up and over roof tops
calling it a day.

Rain is the way it ends
and begins again
in this land of green mansions.

The Weight of Water

A watermarked sun
in a gray silk sky
the field heavy with mist
every web and reed
bent low with its weight
the earth soaked, slick
the light turns silver to sepia
etching the edges
of anything green to gold.
It is morning
it is morning on an island
and we wander back
as the mist rises off the field
releases its hold on time
resets the clock to another day.

At the Edge of the World

Fog blankets the bay.

    A single boat in mid-air

no horizon visible.

    Overhead

gulls knit the sky together.

One

Beetle wings pulsate
to the rodent rhythm heartbeat
of a vole underground.

In the pond's center,
a heron,
bright yellow eye diverted
an instant as I passed
beneath his reed shadow.
A school of minnows
slip quickly down into the muck.

Silken threads overhead
catch my coat
tearing loose the delicate symmetry
of an orb weaver's work.
In a moment she begins
to digest and spin
the damaged threads anew.
Nothing here is wasted.

(One continued)

It is easy to see
in this beautiful chaos
how we are all connected
wing to heart
leaf to root
predator to prey.

But beyond these green boarders we
cannot hear, cannot see, cannot feel
how one touch of the web
changes everything.
So much is formed and reformed
without our notice.
So much we notice
is only an illusion.

Sunrise on Fisher Pond

Gone early to the pond
before the great blue heron
uncoils his snake-neck
and the osprey shakes dew
from her feathered mantle
opens one bold eye
alert for silver scales.

Eos, winged and filled with desire
swells the eastern sky.
The seam of night tears open
spilling golden light as the sun rises
and the music of life rises with it.

Afterwards
I head home and try to hold
what can't be
with imperfect words.

Form Follows Function

This flight feather
loosed from the wing of a Steller's jay
spiraled down in its own flight pattern
to land at my feet
iridescent cobalt blue perfection
shaped to its aerial purpose
grounded but still beautiful.

Whatever is useful
becomes beautiful in its duty
and loosed or laid down
still holds its inner purpose.
No one sees a feather
that does not think of flight
and no one sees a sword
that does not think of blood.

The Lives of Stones

Lichen covered stones
erratics cast by glaciers
what the ice abandoned
remains a green hope.

Nearby, Judd Creek
shapes and scours small stones
for salmon to bury her eggs.

The sea below ripples and rolls
great God handfuls of beach
in a single tide
moves a mountain of stones
in just a winter of time.

The mountain
her stone heart molten and ice covered
beats to the rhythm of geologic time
until her heart breaks and bursts through
the expectant air.

I want to be Lost

I want to be lost
in the branches of the madrone
where the little kingfisher
has taken his stand
day after day by the shore
clattering in his big voice
diving into the sea
and back again.

Stone and Bone

I want to become a stone
in this meandering river
large enough
to hold my place through spring floods
small enough
for a returning salmon to consider
nose me gently before struggling
a little further upstream
where she will dig into lighter gravel
a nest for her bright orange eggs
attracting the blood-colored males
already on their way to death
until both, open-mouthed
mix eggs and seed together.
And after she covers each nest
no longer able to resist
the relentless downstream current
as it carries her spent body gently
back over hard-won riffled river bottom
to be the last place she rests
stone and bone together
bleached white and worn
with weather, water, and time
inanimate, un-noticed, dreaming.

(Stone and Bone continued)

One molten, born in a river of fire
cooled to stillness by a river of ice.
The other, a silver sea traveler
until natal desire compels her
into sinuous red light.

Hold a Stone

Feel the smooth dense weight
in the palm of your hand
listen to the stillness--
It was once a river of sand
It was once molten lava
hardened by time or temperature
made smooth by waves and tide
into this small shape of a human heart.

Listen to the stillness--
the tic tock of our hearts, our time
is not there.
If stone has a beat
it is timed to the rhythm of the earth
in sync with the universe
and music of the stars.

Hold a leaf.

What I See / What I Hear

Hiking the upper trail
crowned by Western hemlocks
sinuous roots embrace
old cedar stumps
that still show ax scars
from centuries ago
cut by an alien species
bent of destruction.

The forest voices
sing a re-vivifying song
to the seedlings that grow
to such heights
from the dead
like Horus, skyward

On the Trail this Morning (for Anne)

From a distance
a poet I know stood still and silent
staring down at a patch of salal
the cold surrounded the two of us
fogged us together.

She looked up and said simply,
"brown wren."
and there it was, small and dark
mouse-colored, plush
puffed up for warmth
against the chill air
close to the earth.

Come Early

to the pond
where the night hunters
are settling in
wings tucked
blood and flesh
cleaned from beaks and talons.
Come early
for the frog people
voicing their opinions
and the Great Blue Heron
waiting with remarkable patience
for the first slicked green body
to emerge.
Come, Come
for the weaver's art
dewy diamond-studded
a trap for prey.
Come early
and you will see
the sun's first kiss
over the dark waters
creates a path of light
from sky to shore.
This is not to be missed
and it happens
every day here!

How can I feel Uninspired?

Walking the trail
where moss-coated maple trees
shimmer with the last rain
under a new sun
and Douglas firs reach skyward
a hundred feet or more.
Exposed cedar roots
the color of blood
weave the rich soil together.
I come with my troubles
to bury them beneath the litter
thick and rich under my feet.
Maybe in time they too will sprout
into something useful
something beautiful.

Mukai Pond Before the Rains

A mosaic of dock and soft rush
bur-reed and wapato
exposed through the long dry summer
waiting for the rains to come
and cover every leaf and stone
for the dragon flies and darners to return
many colored dabblers and divers
and the geese in their black and white attire
the chorus frogs
singing in the season of darkness to come
as the pond rises and widens
we watch the days begin to shrink
bring in the lawn chairs
think about a fire.

A Thousand Moons

Loons

Just before sundown
I heard a loon trilling
unmistakable and magical
as it always is and predictable
always in spring.
A year ago I could not bear it
and how strange today
the sound is sweet again
without the bitter.

This Business of Survival

Too often I let my heart slip away
while I go about this business
of survival
not the hawk clean kill kind
but the petty, papery kind
where I lose myself inside a maze
of obligations and emails
but this morning a friend and I
(he who never leaves his heart
anywhere but inside his small grey self)
will wander to the pond
and around and into the wood
listen for raven and crow
watch for the osprey to circle overhead
then I can go back
to this business of survival
just a little more in love with the world.

Transpiration

This morning
the fog uncurled its fingers
from the cedar branches
and the trees breathed mist
warmed by the sun
transpiring
creating
the very air I breathed.

Drift I

Walking the beach this morning
away from the catastrophe
watching Caspian Terns hunting the drift
I found myself seeking those
small treasures, a welk shell, sea glass
a perfect molted crab shell.
For a while, the world is calm
And nothing is out of balance
I know this is temporary
but it is also true.

Drift II

This bay is nothing like the sea
with crashing waves and violence.
It has become tamed by geology
and time
its waters slowed and muted
into narrow throats
by ancient glaciers.

I hear the sea birds calling
one to another
and sometimes the sound
of a train on the mainland
rarely waves on shore.

Killdeers skitter along the drift
indiscriminate nesting habits
require noise and feints
to distract predators.
The gulls own the sandspit
further down the beach
waiting for a careless clam
to show its siphon.

Drift III

So much commerce goes on
beneath and above the shore
sand dollars, cockles, and clams
so much life under every step.
Low tide anemones
hang flaccid off the pilings.
In this sorry state
no one is reminded
of their name sake flowers
until the tide turns
on its diurnal moon path
and like the moon herself
they rise
tentacles reaching upward
open-faced, blooming.

A Thousand Moons

Moon jellies dance
a pulsing polka
in time with the tides
round like their namesake
glow phosphorescent
a thousand moons
in the dark water.

Following the Drift

From this beach
the shore bends to the will
of diurnal tides in the Salish Sea
that roll past our small island
driving drift and debris alike onshore
where we wander and wonder
the dog and I
at crab parts and plastic pieces
so similar in color and frequency
though one will eventually
succumb to wind, weather, and tide.
The other remains long past its usefulness
if it ever had any.
The dog's interest and mine
are curiosity
but I do not taste or chase
just observe, sometimes collect
my pockets are always full
sometimes sand sifts
through my dreams.

Between

The ferry's turbines
sound like steel drums
a pod of Orcas sleek by
and a flock of flightless tourists
run portside, cameras at the ready
I sit and think about
what shore I am bound
caught between two islands
in different latitudes.

I think about the Orcas
those beautiful killers
mythologized in films and stories
then remembered the dark shadows
of dolphins beneath our small outriggers
on the way to bat island
in Sulawesi, Indonesia
half a world away.
Someday I should
get off this boat, plant a flag
take a stand
make a choice.

Star Craft

The wind is calm
and the bay a mirror
for the moon
when the heron calls me awake
I light the candles
ring the bowl
find my seat.
Stillness carries its own wind
rustling through my thoughts
loosening the moorings
chafing the lines little by little
there is no rudder or sail
on her own my craft is crafty
bent on open water
and something indefinable
behind the stars.

Red Tide

View from the shore below
a swath of rust red
the color of dried blood
a toxic soup of micro-organisms
floating in on the tide
more prevalent each passing year
as the seas warm and rise.
I hurry on past the view of Mount Rainier
past the goat farm and what remains
of paradise fossilized in an amber sunrise.

At the Lighthouse

Two harbor seals
an adult and a pup
hauled out on the beach
we back track so as not to disturb them.

Fishing boats offshore
the light house eye is blind these days
the power to its Fresnel lens shut off
years ago
but in the morning light
It gleams on its own
Two people fish from the shore
A meditation.

After reading Mary Oliver's 'Thirst' and Pondering Faith

Does it matter
how she came to faith
but loving her as I do
or loving her words
having never met
her words have pulled at my heart
my shrunken little heart for years.

I think love, the same kind of love
that brought me to despair
brought her to despair
and then to her faith.
My faith is watered wine
without enough punch or fire
to make the effort worth the fall.

I tried the alter and bowl
then followed her words into the open fields
on the long trail by the dark pond
I followed as a supplicant
after a saint.
Perhaps she would be appalled by this.
But I know light
when it dawns on me.

www.ingramcontent.com/pod-product-compliance
Lightning Source LLC
Chambersburg PA
CBHW051932240626
47153CB00004B/1467